ISBN: 978-1-66780-421-7

Photos courtesy of:
(in order of appearance)

Mike Schoepp
Nathan Dumlao
Jeremy Bishop
Kenrick Mills
Aaron Burden
Ulysse Pointcheval
Wolfgang Hasselmann

Book Cover Design by Kelly Carey.
https://kellycareydesign.com/

This book is dedicated to Susan Schoepp, my wife, living for so much and to lose her to kidney disease, has forever altered my journey. We each meant the world to each other.

I remember the first day of our honeymoon in Maui, Susan stood under a double rainbow holding a sunflower. The path that follows the rainbow will find you when you are lost.

With you ... always with me.

Table of Contents

Faith

To feel so much as shoulders grow weary ...
and long to lose the depth of care and worry.

Days are endless, as time will dart.
The sun fades away and falls apart.

To see more beyond than you can grasp...
may find a tone of subtleness which will last.

So reach deep within to find what you need ...
and the Lords' blessing will guide you indeed.

.

Close By

Here with Sue quite a while.
Steps taken seem like a mile.

I have lost myself without much esteem.
To lose a part of myself was not my dream.

It is only for kindness I covet, then fall ...
from the one who is above it all.

The thought of what could be ...
here under my Christmas tree.

A simple wish of a memory,
could reveal such a story.

A lack of focus is not sorry.
We do not win to find glory.

Dreams

I will find strength where meaning is not clear...
to find her even when she does not care.

She often gets lost and does not prepare ...
for losing her is more than I can bear.

And for the day as it sometimes seems.
I only really see her in my dreams.

6

Her World

I think to myself as I sit in my chair ...
a thought or two as I touch my hair.

No embrace of life or even a care.
We can see what we hope to hear ...

For all we love it is free of fear...
as parts of myself start to tear...

In pieces of life that is hard to bear ...
then she rides in the sky on her white mare.

8

Prayer

Most times it does help to pray ...
that things will go alright and be okay.

Somehow you make it through each day ...
while caring for your wife in every way.

When all you can do is never the best ...
Some times for others and not the rest.

To covet more then you find ...
will only leave us far behind.

It is not without strength from within ...
but more a gift unique to our kin.

It allows us to see perspective ...
in all that we do and give...

To accept things and just let live ...
to reveal more than one can gauge.

10

Shades of Hope

Go to dialysis and eat.
Take your meds and defeat ...

all that breaks down inside.
It is your choice, you must decide

You can do it.

We will together ...
when weighted souls lift to a feather.

Feeling overwhelmed from all ...
Lord, cradle us not to fall.

Do not give up hope as you go along ...
with faith in God, you will be strong.

12

Strength

I try somehow to express the pain and sorrow ...
knowing it will last for more than tomorrow.

I want not for myself but to shine for her ...
as a solid person beyond what can endure.

Following these roads end up much the same.
the short, windy ones are so hard to tame.

The Lord gives answers to what we pray ...
if we are unselfish in our deeds of the day.

His hand rugged and lined with creases ...
picks us up before we all go to pieces.

14

Susan

You must be so lost inside and how.
Do not be scared, hold on right now.

You will pull through, you are fearless.
You have us, our love is peerless.

We all miss you and are out of kilter.
Feelings are tough to block and filter.

You are so precious and will know ...
that our support will help you grow.

A shower of goodness will come to be.
Our dogs are waiting for you and me.

Along the path that brings you home ...
comes strength to you in this poem.

16

The Eyes of my Dogs

They perceive things in ways we do not see ...
to find safety and comfort to just let things be.

When they are scared and bark with each other ...
they will be blessed by the love of their mother.

The dedication provided to those she endures ...
has nurtured our family for so many years.

It is a miracle to see them play and grow ...
with all the love and loyalty they show.

When they cuddle with you each night ...
then everything seems to be all right.

18

Another Time

An amazing world of marine ...
where all is calm and serene.

Close memories to share ...
are ocean birds of a pair.

Boats that are two of a kind ...
follow one and stay behind.

A buoy stays afloat to find ...
canoes turn, twist and bind.

Cool trade winds fill the sail ...
water topped a whale's tail.

It waves and then descends ...
to be with sea life friends.

20

Mountain Star

To feel the air so crisp and thin ...
valleys echo the drop of a pin.

The snow is so soft and plush.
Sun sparkles and turns to blush.

Some cool breezes have a sway ...
and are felt throughout the day.

Overlooking these hills appear ...
clustered clouds that are near.

Evening dawn paints the sky ...
beauty that makes you sigh.

Moonlit mountains not too far.
Keep reaching for your star.

22

24

Rain and Sea

You hear soft drizzle of the rain ...
brushing off tops of sugar cane.

The droplets on the window pane ...
coat the wood, enhance the grain.

When the water has no place to go ...
it can feel trapped, like the snow.

A crisp breeze by the ocean ...
puffs of briny air in the potion.

The sea waves its crest in sets of seven ...
before the mist evaporates to heaven.

Far away, on the horizon sky ...
are clouds that want to cry.

The warm rays of the sun ...
soon bring smiles to everyone.

26

Seasons

Mother Nature knows what we can only guess.
Spring should be here in a few weeks or less.

It may be sooner, but no one will stress.
Fall is my favorite as is time to confess.

We will be eating turkey and dressing ...
and trying to find our own blessing.

Summer is warmer a few months in between.
What is taken for granted cannot be unseen.

Days are harsh in the winter.
Cold frost bites like a splinter.

We hang on for unknown reasons.
Love carries us through the seasons.

28

Waves

They break in sets of seven.
riding atop is close to heaven.

In comes a fresh spectacular mist ...
with air so light and its spray a crest.

Somewhere in between the sets ...
brings me to a time with no regrets.

Paddling along and counting the strokes ...
having ono potluck with local folks.

An age not so far away in pieces and parts ...
of a culture we hold so dear to our hearts.

Mahalo nui loa all the way.
Aloha in each and every day.

30

Fall

Pretty soon Fall will be here.
It is my favorite time of the year.

A curiousity more than a wonder...
it is fun to watch the thunder.

It is when the leaves show their hues ...
soft crayon colors to cure your blues.

Whistling sounds of a gentle breeze ...
awakens the sun to chase off the freeze.

32

Who We Are

The family is built like a strong tree.
It has leaves and branches for us to see.

The memories shared by us, a little by me...
have shown us the ways to set our souls free.

We know the reason why we never lose sight ...
of various ways we can make our lives right.

We must never give up, but always fight ...
to keep us together and always tight.

You won't always see a shining bright star.
Just remember we should be who we are.

Here and now I sincerely say to you.
To have loyalty is to always be true.

It is the mainframe of trust.
For this we follow, oh we must ...

We learn to somehow let live.
Then we find the patience to give.

If we are good and do our best ...
then love will take care of the rest.

34

36

Willful

A shouldered burden lifted in his care.
Ask for strength, he will always be near.

One who can see their path along the way ...
should not be caught up or led astray ...

with any deception of reality on their road ...
or to change their life for fear of goad.

Only time can show us what is to come.
We keep the loyalty to the family we are from.

38

Supermoms

She is always there ...
anytime and anywhere.

Her unconditional love is kind.
It is pretty easy for us to find.

She shares special moments and times ...
reading us stories and nursery rhymes.

She embraces us when we grieve ...
holding our tears 'til they retrieve.

With much guidance and direction ...
comes reinforcement and protection.

She races across the road to save ...
a child from speeding cars, so brave.

Her dedication keeps the family together ...
with true balance and grace of a feather.

She rescues one trapped underwater ...
A new chance for someone's daughter.

She was strong for her baby last year ...
by saving his life and giving him care.

Our supermoms are here forever ...
With us on our journey to endeavor.

40

Rocky Road

It is what makes me happy to see my family ...
for the simple reason is that I can just be me.

An awe-inspiring day we may rarely see ...
usually these things cannot set us free.

We must hold close to us what is dear ...
when we trust we move beyond the fear.

Then things usually change all at once.
Spoken words are less than a hunch.

For I always rolled with the punches.
I send my love to you all in bunches.

42

Reflections of Christmas

You sit by the fireplace with your dog …
reading a book as you toss on a log.

Finding calm in words and rhyme …
brings memories of another time.

An angel touched our heart …
and kept it from falling apart.

As a toddler so young in years …
waiting for Santa and reindeers.

Often you will get a tan …
If you build a snowman.

Unless the sun has gone to rest …
behind clouds of cotton nest.

Now we gather and play games …
and call out each other's names.

You know what Christmas is about …
being with family leaves no doubt.

A New Year

We went through a lot of changes
and turned a lot of pages.

Trapped in these cages ...
sorting through our last rages.

Finding a purpose in a different way ...
and just transcending through the day.

Took a ride Sunday in the new year ...
drove in roads often visited by deer.

Sun was lost soon before being greeted ...
by family to keep me from feeling defeated.

We shared the love and kindness we know ...
with one another and it made the night glow.

In such a magical way you feel ...
nothing else could be more real.

The memory becomes a part of me ...
much like the spirit of our family tree.

46

Music in Me

A gift shared by mom, so fond ...
music remains a common bond.

Remembering years of childhood ...
spinning records made it good.

Words of wisdom to comprehend ...
instruments create notes to send.

The soothing harmony in a song ...
fades away before long.

Lyrics that we sometimes recall ...
making us stand proud and tall.

48

Growing Up

We saw animals at the SF Zoo all the time ...
nights slumbered by a nursery rhyme.

We had great costumes at Halloween.
When spring arrives we wore green.

At Christmas-time we carried our tree ...
careful to not shake the bristles free.

We learned about the different places ...
the culture of people and their races.

We got married and started our lives ...
with the love of husbands and wives.

Seeing youth through children's eyes ...
is such beauty, one you cannot mize.

.

Family Tree

Here is a seed that holds within it a story ...
wanting to reveal anything not of glory.

The leaves reach out to the sunshine ...
yearning for everything to be fine.

Then it seems to grow in its own way.
It could not find balance for today.

In all that we see in what nature provides ...
we tend to lose focus of all of its sides.

Then much closer to the reach ...
you find life has more to teach.

The tree has grown branches all strong ...
to show us at times where we belong.

In its earthy wholeness we found ...
where our family's love is bound.

52

Another Year

We have found our way through the end of the year...

and managed so much to avoid feeling the fear.
Many challenges bring us more than we can bear.

Our minds tend to hibernate moments of the day.
We become sharper to focus on more than we may.

Oh, the timeless months passed as they did ...
bringing subtle calmness beyond all that we bid.

In the new year we will be stronger and seek ...
more family goodness just like last week.

54

Stars and Stripes

Such a special day in every way.

Seeing countryside beauty by one ...
played scrabble and had some fun.

With family precious to me ...
moments of time to feel free.

Festive mood and tones ...
ever-lasting yummy rib bones ...

Driving home was quite strange ...
things became more out of range.

The rugged jalopy did search ...
soon to stray from its perch.

Car never stalled on the road ...
how saved from trouble mode?

Need to check the engine code ...
no worry – will carry the load.

Life can never be tragic ...
it rests within such magic.

Gracefully held in God's hand ...
not to ponder or understand.

56

58

Gift of Love

The part of life we do not know ...
remains a mystery as we grow.

Pieces of the moon will show ...
as tides sway from high to low.

Visions of soft clouds so high ...
ones you can reach in the sky.

No matter how hard we try ...
sometimes it is better to cry.

With memories in our heart ...
bonded together, never apart.

Feeling Life

Have you ever gone through the day ...
where much is heavy along the way?

Feeling emotions that want to stay ...
when they wither it will be okay.

Sometimes in life, so dearly we pay ...
for loud projections with little to say.

Make time to laugh and play ...
to see the wings of a baby jay.

The sun chases the clouds in May ...
after a misty cry, no longer gray.

62

Here with You

You are loved from the start ...

hugging me to warm my heart.
Why did you leave us both apart?

Missing you so much too ...
feeling so lost in what to do.

Those happy moments in our years ...
will cherish memories to soften tears.

Talking to you every day ...
feels good in every way.

You were crying to me one night ...
to reach out and hold you tight.

When kissed with all goodbyes ...
leaving with kindness in your eyes.

The gift you gave for one can see ...
your blessed spirit will always be.

64

Keeping it Together

Where it starts do we know?
see the tickets to the show.

Flipping peanut shells about.
Hoping the game is not a rout.

Baseball is strange in its own way.
In the park we watch them play.

In a soft grassy field of dreams ...
life is mostly not what it seems.

Imagination creates its own mind.
Illusions are mirrors for us to find.

Then when things seem all right ...
we keep together with all might.

Peaceful Reflection

In time a place far away ...
here gentle palms sway.

Not in a dream, but so serene ...
baby turtles from the marine.

Ocean current brings new life ...
and takes the ashes of my wife.

Now being where she loves ...
clouds feathered like doves.

Over the rainbow so clear ...
misty sky drops a tear.

Though always near ...
deeply missed throughout the year.

68

Lost in Myself

One can write often about how they feel ...
and can gain perception to what is real.

Being on a merry-go-round so long ...
it is easy to lose the passion in your song.

Dreams and hopes go by the wayside.
Everything else just gets lost in the tide.

I see so much strength in my family.
It is what gives me inspiration to see.

They bring the love that sets me free ...
so that I can have fun and just be me.

72

Valentine

We came together as good friends.
We do see this is where it begins.

I feel her love in my heart ...
a wonderful place for us to start.

Through much patience she has grown ...
from all the strength she has shown.

As I gaze into her eyes of brown ...
a vision of gentle love I've found.

Like the sun, my body warms ...
when I hold her in my arms.

With the warmth that is felt ...
even on a cold day I still melt.

This I saw with so much pride ...
that soon she will be my bride.

She takes my hand and walks with me ...
together and forever we will be free.

Thoughts

Pondering why times are so tough.
Things okay, maybe not quite enough.

No vision from some crystal ball ...
to finally find where we may fall.

The afternoon cast of shadows on the wall ...
make shimmers of images dance to their call.

Water flowing on low side of stream ...
froths with air to resemble cream.

Was not for what it would seem ...
merely only in some kind of dream.

76

Time Rhyme

Seconds become a minute ...
before our minds are really in it.

The hour to come will bring ...
the subtleness of a soft hymn.

The hours in a day to follow ...
seems endless and hollow.

Days that form the week ...
often reveal more than we seek.

Weeks are a month fast.
How long will it last?

Moving into the year not immune to fear.
Soon we will be lost in time, rhythm and rhyme.

78

True Colors

Open your way to emotions ...
so cares drift to the oceans.

Seek to crest a sixth wave.
Keep a path so brave.

Within today we will grow ...
as spirit brings life aglow.

The sea of green looks blue ...
some kind of shade or hue.

Happiness soon will tower ...
smiling face on a sunflower.

.

Peaks and Valleys

Always working to reach our peak ...
in health and strength, never meek.

Sometimes we can find what we seek ...
simple joy and kindness in our week.

The sun rides low in the valley ...
for sparkling bits of light to rally.

Virus puts us in a dark alley ...
taking too many lives to tally.

Most of our earth is in deep pain.
Seeds still come up with the rain.

Fields of gold in the hollow ...
reveals a smooth path to follow.

82

Never Alone

Sometime in the month of May ...
the shore sparkled a moon's ray.

The night before our wedding day ...
all became clear, no longer gray.

When it was time to give her away ...
she joined my heart to always stay.

Followed a rainbow to Napili Bay ...
watching dolphins and turtles play.

In loving memories she seems to say ...
you can reach me when you pray.

.

.

Happy Place

Stay focused on a small dream.
Follow the creek, find a stream.

Go to the lake or the coast.
Find a place you love most.

Walking on a sandy beach ...
a gentle breeze at our reach.

Time to surrender your care ...
to those memories we share.

The rainbow in the morning sky ...
Shows you'll never say goodbye.

88

.

Your Rainbow

Life is not served on platters.
It humbles us more than flatters.

Stalled upwind, sail in tatters ...
being there when it matters.

Sparkles of light at sunset ...
under horizon not just yet.

Sky falls in to darkness so calm.
Ocean breeze whispers a psalm.

Subtle reflections of the moon ...
glow softly, enhances the tune.

Then tomorrow a mist by noon ...
will show me your rainbow soon.

.

Letting Go

Coveting with all might ...
unwilling to give up fight.

One day came a light.
Passing was her right.

Such visions in mind ...
gentle spirit will find.

Here in this empty chair ...
moonlight makes us stare.

Riding on velvet mare ...
image fades from air...

leaving life much to bear.
Loving soul will always fare.

92

Mindful Path

Milk soon boils to steam ...
then evaporates to cream.

In your eye I saw a gleam ...
one to define your dream.

Waking up to what is real.
Your life, no one can steal.

In thoughts, how you feel ...
is when you start to heal.

Putting effort into things ...
motivation, what it brings.

Carrying upon those wings ....
hope over whatever stings.

When picture becomes clear ...
you move on and shed fear.

Focusing what you endure ...
finds goodness in the year.

Partly Whole

Loneliness absence of sense ...
emptiness becomes immense.

Staying within much of the time ...
searching for the one sublime.

Finding comfort in rhyme ...
lyrics to read or mime.

In ground like a mole ...
a flat rock will not roll.

Life remains partly whole ...
until love finds the soul.

Sunshine Daydream

Sometimes it seems there are no eyes around ...
when being alone feels a bit more sound.

It could not be heard for sense abound ...
getting lost a bit before we are found.

To meditate in moments each day ...
permits the sun to find its way.

The rain cries puddles beyond ...
tears gather to form a pond.

In between the balance of the two ...
will be a rainbow of such hue ...

as I send all of my love to you.

Torn Pages

Happiness is skiing and playing ball,
being with family and standing tall.

Kindness brings smiles for sure ...
always times so simple and pure.

Finding diversions around the house ...
setting traps for an occasional mouse.

Now days are spent dedicated to one ...
who seldom seems to have much fun.

Working on a ramp for chair out back.
tweeting with birds having a snack.

Baby sparrow once would stay ...
soon to fly and find her way.

100

Always Remember

Our leader's empathy seems to lack ...
with careless direction, nothing to back.

Callously going through the motion ...
making claim for a miracle potion.

The heroes in this true despair ...
are the selfless angels of healthcare.

In our prayers of those we lost ...
are families and lives it will cost.

A future path soon to show ...
different than what we know.

102

Maile

Maile is a flower of Hawaiian royal ...
memories sweet, she was so loyal.

She sometimes hopped like a bunny ...
and looked like a bear eating honey.

Charlie and Lucie are feeling so sad.
Maile was a little sister they never had.

Losing you Maile has taken its toll.
We will find you again, it is our goal.

Your gentle spirit and brave soul ...
pieces our heart, makes it whole.

104

Circus Angel

The Bengal tiger in his cage ...
jumped up with eyes of rage.

All senses were heightened ...
quite frazzled and frightened.

He could not let me in for a ride ...
but his fear stayed locked inside.

Sometimes you play the clown ...
laughing to not feel so down.

Along the way you learn to juggle ...
tools to carry you through the struggle.

An angel took me under wing ...
touched my soul and taught me to sing.

Somewhere on land and sea ...
finding a worthy life for me.

106

108

Searching

Life develops from root and seed ...
grows to provide for all to feed.

It could have been for all but beyond a reach ...
and not fall from the birch grabbing a peach.

Blessings for us all and soon to follow ...
hold strong through the deep or hollow.

May our paths be less rugged as ever ...
in search of step to seek what is clever.

Things you work hard for, it would seem ...
can be answered in a prayer or dream.

In goodness we feel warmth and a light glow ...
as worries drift from what we used to know.

Superstar

You have a heart so young.
In joy a rhythm will be sung.

When you find who you are ...
be confident of yourself, to raise the bar.

It is because you are a shining star ...
very few know how to keep the par.

Your inspiration guides me to and afar.

.

Heartful

Went to the canyon just this week ...
in search of someone to seek.

Walking towards pine creek ...
just far enough for a peek.

Off the trail, the smooth part ...
outlines the image of a heart.

There rests her spirit and love ...
always watching from above.

Her smiling face like a star.
Her strength takes us far.

The warmth and kindness you bring ...
make the flowers bloom in the spring.

The gentle softness of a feather ...
fond memories shared together.

114

Puzzle of Life

Life is more a puzzle than a riddle ...
hoping the ends will find the middle.

Pieces of life are jagged and rough.
The hidden ones will make it touch.

There are many steps along the way.
Unfocused moments may confuse the day.

When it comes together in a groove ...
your image will be clear and smooth.

.

Acknowledgements

Thank you to my father, Hank for his encouragement and support in providing a path for me to follow,

Thank you to my niece, Kelly Carey, who as a very talented graphic artist has created the cover art for this book.

A special thanks to my sister, Caroline Carey, who has put together everything that is needed for this book and continues to give strength, hope and direction on this journey.